Murals of Lassen County

Major sponsorships provided by

City of Susanville
Bank of America
Plumas Bank
Tri-Counties Bank
U.S. Forest Service
California State Fair, 1998
  (Counties Exhibit Award for Lassen County)
ComPAC (Community Planning and Advisory
  Council)
Operational Energy Corporation

Lassen County Cattlemen and Cattlewomen
Sierra Pacific Industries
Pacific EZ Soft
California Correctional Center
Paul Schlotterbeck
Charles and Corrine Reed
Will and Colleen Thorn
Lassen County Arts Council

Copyright © 2008 by Lassen County Arts Council
ISBN: 0-9768871-0-X

Printed in China

Published in association with Word Dancer Press
Sanger, California
800-497-4909.

Introduction

THE ODYSSEY Of DEFINED THINGS

Our community is losing its members-
Blackbirds, drifting off into the sky,
Their volumes of light left behind.
For we who subsist in text, story or paint,
There is continuity in this, in this passing.
For what are we but the framework
Of the defined, articulated in momentary time?
The rueful hurt of it all, the face that once lit
A corsage of other faces, now lights candle - stars

Dianna Henning
Petra Rees

This book is dedicated to the memory of Ben Barker, whose vision and initiative made it a reality.

Introduction

In the early 1980's, local college art teacher Ben Barker returned to Susanville from a trip to a small town in British Columbia that was filled with historic murals. Ben was inspired by what he had seen; he and others convinced Susanville's city leaders to begin Susanville's own Historic Mural Project, as a way of revitalizing the uptown area of Susanville.

The events and characters depicted in Lassen County's murals help to explain the unique character of this place. Susanville lies at the junction of mountains and high desert, where several distinct native cultures intersected, where pioneer settlers brought ranching and logging, giving way in modern times to tourism and recreation. The unique cultures and characters who came together here are depicted in the murals; this public art gives residents and visitors alike a sense of the history that made Susanville the special place that it is today.

As pieces of public art, murals exist on several levels at once. They blend with their geographical environment, transforming it and giving it new dimensions. Murals are also social and historical narratives that record important events and indicate their cultural significance.

The Mural Project is a demonstration of what can happen when a community comes together, creates a common vision, and works together to make that vision a reality. In the late 1980's, community meetings helped to create broad-based support for the project. Financial support came from the California Arts Council, the Lassen County Arts Council, the City of Susanville, and many local businesses, organizations, and agencies. Each new supporter has helped to enhance and broaden the community vision for the Murals Project.

Contents

Contents

Lassen County Profile

California

Lassen County is a land of wide open spaces and sweeping vistas. It is the third largest county in land area in California, yet one of the smallest in population. Its 4,547 square miles of varied terrain includes high desert, snowcapped peaks, vast agricultural valleys, grassy meadows, and lush forests. Spring, summer, fall and winter offer seasonal diversity and excitement. Average temperatures range from 28 degrees in winter to 93 degrees in summer.

Lassen County provided plentiful natural resources for our early settlers; today, it is a popular destination for hunters and fishermen, hikers, and bicyclists, and all who seek a quieter, less-hurried pace of life.

Three early pioneer routes, the Nobles Trail, The Beckworth Trail, and the Lassen Trail, brought early settlers into and through Lassen County. Trail markers and other historic sites continue to bring travelers to the area.

Historically a logging and farming community, agricultural producers continue to support the local economy. In 2001, for example, Lassen County's total agricultural production was valued at over 43 million dollars.

In addition to timber, livestock, alfalfa, and other hay production, agricultural producers have diversified into producing such commodities as alfalfa seed, garlic, strawberry nursery stock, wild rice, and mint for oil production.

State and Federal Government are prominent economic sectors in Lassen County: Two of California's 28 state prisons are located in Lassen County, and they are major employers. Lassen National Forest covers much of Lassen County, and also accounts for significant State and Federal employment. The 2000 census shows public administration employment in Lassen County as 26.9 percent of the total, compared to 4.5 percent in that same sector statewide. Lassen Community College is also a significant State government employer.

❶ Our Ancestors, Our Future

"Our Ancestors, Our Future," 42'W x 18'H, 1999
Artist: Jean La Marr, Assistant: Jack Malotte
Location: Odd Fellows Building, NE Corner of Main & Lassen, Susanville, CA

Humans have lived in the area now know as Lassen County for eight to ten thousand years—since the time of the last ice age. In this mural, Jean LaMarr and Jack Malotte depict prominent Native American figures of the nineteenth and twentieth centuries.

8

Murals can be social and historical statements. By recognizing important figures in the history of a culture, the current generation pays tribute to its ancestors.

Chief Winnemucca

CHIEF WINNEMUCCA

Chief Winnemucca, a Paiute, was a peace seeker. With Isaac Roop, he signed a treaty between the settlers and Native Americans in the Honey Lake Valley.

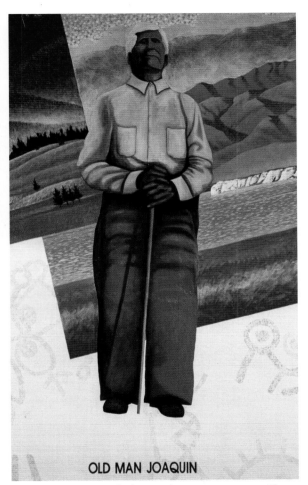

OLD MAN JOAQUIN

Old Man Joaquin's native name was Sau Wa-Be, which means "sagebrush." He lived near Eagle Lake and had many daughters. Today, many of his descendents live at the Susanville Rancheria.

9

Our Ancestors, Our Future

A background of petroglyphs suggests the distant past—a world of lost images and lives that existed long before Europeans came to this country. The work is both serious and hopeful, infused with the colors of Lassen County—the deep indigo of sunset, the subtle shades of the high desert, and the glitter of frost in winter. Old and new blends into a vision of local people and the land that formed them.

SUSIE EVANS

MAUDE SAILORS

GRACE MIKE GUITIEREZ

Susie Evans, a medicine woman and a basket weaver, passed stories on to Leonard Lowry, who passed them on to the next generations.

Maude Sailors began working at age 10 on ranches. She later worked at the sawmill and as a fork lift operator.

Grace Mike Guitierez often visited with friends under the store awning next to this mural. She represented her tribe in local, state, and national government.

10

TOMMY TUCKER

Tommy Tucker was the first Lassen County man to die in World War I; he is buried in the Susanville Cemetery.

Jean La Marr first became interested in mural work in the 1970's while attending UC Berkeley as an art major. She saw the mock-up for a mural that was to be painted in an Oakland park and became upset because of the degrading images of Native Americans that it contained. She helped in getting that project stopped, and went on to become a mural painter herself.

Jean was born and raised in Susanville. Her career has taken her across America, from the National Museum of the American Indian at the Smithsonian to the New York Museum of Modern Art. Her prints have been shown in galleries and museums around the United States and Europe, and her murals have been recognized nationally.

"Creating Her History," 50'Wx15'H, 1993
Artist: Judith Lowry, Assistants: Justine and Chelsea Clark
Location: Doyle Motors Building, 611 Main Street, Susanville, CA

In "Creating Her History," Judith Lowry pays tribute to the women of Lassen County by representing two different cultures that have been important in the county's history, while symbolizing the ideas of birth and regeneration.

The mural's central European figure, Mrs. Potter, was the local midwife for many years. Opposite her is a native woman of the Bear Dance, an annual spring ceremony. The old storyteller on the right illustrates the oral tradition of the older generation passing on their history to the younger. The counterpart to this storyteller is the figure of Miss Heavner, who taught for many years in Susanville. Miss Heavner, who was 92 at the time this mural was painted, is depicted with her 1926 kindergarten class.

The plants which border the mural are a combination of indigenous and introduced species, representing both the changes in the area over time and the way new species and old adapt and learn to live together. Through the mural runs the Susan River, pulling the native and pioneer women together even as it emphasizes their separate roles in forming the history of Lassen County. The river is a gathering place in Lowry's mural. Mountain Maidu women gathered willows along the river to weave baskets. Pioneer women worked on their quilts. Other figures represent women who worked alongside men on ranches and farms, in lumber camps, and in small mountain towns.

This mural was Lowry's first. Although visiting Los Angeles muralist Arthur Mortimer advised her to use a grid to transfer her design to the wall, Lowry discovered that she could not conform to such a rigid system. "I am more of an intuitive painter. In the end, I went out and bought those big fat chalks that kids use to draw on the sidewalks, and just climbed up there and drew it all freehand. Then I had to paint in the outlines very quickly before the rain came," Judith said.

Judith Anne Lowry received a Master of Arts from California State University, Chico and has also studied photography, painting and sculpture. Her work, shown primarily in California, reflects her diverse cultural heritage. Lowry's own family, a mix of Mountain Maidu and Pit River, has lived in Lassen County since before the arrival of European settlers. Lowry's father was a Susanville native and Mountain Maidu descendant. Her mother is Australian. Much of Lowry's youth was spent in Europe where she learned western classics and listened to her father's tribal stories. Her own work is a blend of western and Native American symbolism.

15

❸ History of Lassen County

"History of Lassen County," 109'W x 12'H, 1983
Artist: Jaquie Cordova
Location: 715 Main St., Susanville, CA (Bank of America parking lot)

The "History of Lassen County" presents a seasonal and period history of the area now known as Lassen County. The mural is divided into 10 vivid panels in which landscape scenes provide the backdrop for the varied cultures that have shaped the history of this unique area.

In panel 1, a Canada goose soars over Goodrich Meadows, with Keddie Ridge in the background. Within the Keddie Range near Westwood are three lakes; Deerheart, Hidden, and Homer. In the foreground of panel one are loggers felling a tree: as the tree falls, it changes from yellow pine to cedar to lodgepole pine. Historically, these three tree species have been the primary resources for area commercial logging and household heating.

① ② ③

In the 2nd panel, a snow goose flies between snow-capped Diamond Mountain and Eagle Lake, the pristine water body that ranks as the second largest natural lake in California. In panel 3, an angler, representing the attraction of recreation in Lassen County's unspoiled surroundings, reels in an Eagle Lake trout while an Osprey flies across the scene clutching his own catch.

17

④ ⑤ ⑥

In panel 4, mallard ducks fly between Eagle Lake and the Nubieber area of north Lassen country, while trucks carrying logs and firewood move down a mountain road. In the foreground a lumberjack prepares to limb a snag, a common early twentieth century practice. In panel 5, a financier inspects progress on railroad construction, commenting on the fine work by a foreman and his crew. In panel 6: Farming, the main industry in the Bieber and Nubieber areas, serves as a backdrop for the prospector and his mule. Though more prevalent in the late 1800's and early 1900's, gold mining has taken place at Hayden Hill as recently as the 1990's.

⑦ ⑧

Panel 7: Three Basque men reflect on the stray calfs that wandered into their sheep heard near Spanish Mountain in the Ravendale area. The images for the shepherds were taken from a photograph used in Donald Garate's Book, <u>From Red Rock to Ravendale</u>. Panel 8: Cattle Ranching has long been a prevelant industry in Lassen County. The ranch landscape transitions the viewer from the high desert of the Ravendale area to the Honey Lake Valley.

⑨

⑩

Panel 9: The attempts to win peace between Europeon settlers and Native Americans in the county are depicted here. The man on the left is Captain William Weatherlow, an 1850's pioneer explorer who came to the area with Susanville's founder, Isaac Roop. On the right is Chief Winnemucca, a Paiute leader of the time.

Panel 10: The Honey Lake Valley serves as backdrop for a Maidu women gathering roots. The Maidus and Paiutes had inhabited this valley for centuries when the first Europeans arrived.

Jacquie Cordova grew up in the Bay Area. She received her MA from the University of California at Berkeley, and while living in San Francisco, she studied with Elmer Bischoff, a distinguished San Francisco teacher and artist, whom she credits for much of her interest in art. After working in many other fields, Jaquie moved to Westwood, California, where she taught in local schools. She eventually decided that her heart was behind a paint brush rather than behind a desk.

Heart is what Jacquie paints into her murals. She takes the time to consider the opinions and concerns of local residents, striving to represent the spirit of the people and the physical attributes of the county before she begins her work. Thanks to her listening skills, Jacquie receives interesting commentary and advice from local historians and "Old Timers."

❹ Pioneer History

"Pioneer History," 72' W x 6' H, 1990
Mentor: Ben Barker
Principal Artists: Kathleen Colvin,
Eileen Stevens, Mary Morphis.
Assistants/Design: Christine Law,
Janice Moseley, Miyako Yoshida,
Miho Ogoshi, Shirley Spenger,
Donna Keator
Location: Inside the Pioneer Restaurant &
Lounge,
724 Main St., Susanville, CA

This large multi-panel mural inhabits the walls of The Pioneer Bar, the oldest business establishment in northeastern California. Like the Pioneer Bar itself, the mural exudes a flavor of the old west with its cowboys and covered wagons, stagecoach and cattle. The front of the building looks much the same today.

Ben Barker mentored several student interns in the execution of this work, and the unique visions of the different artists comes through in many personal, individual touches. In fact, one of the student artists rendered Ben Barker leaning on a walking stick next to a stack of logs.

The stagecoach appears in the mural because Barker had just been commissioned to paint a mural of a stagecoach in Greenville, CA and wanted to use the mural "Pioneer History" as a testing ground.

Ben Barker

22

The owner of The Pioneer, Bill Bayer, is depicted at the edge of the forest reading a history book while several mule deer look on. Bayer's brothers also appear on top of a wagon. The men in black suits shown in the foreground of the bottom panel represent the Red River Lumber Company logging bosses.

⑤ Mountain Meadows Reservoir

"Walker Lake," 120'W x 22'H, 1994
Artist: Jacqueline Cordova
Location: 323 Birch St., Westwood, CA

In 1912 the town of Westwood, 25 miles west of Susanville, was established on the edge of Mountain Meadows. It was the company town for the Red River Lumber Company's mill and had an extensive railroad and truck logging network throughout the region. In 1944 the company sold its plant and town to the Fruit Growers Supply Company.

Mountain Meadows Reservoir, a sanctuary for many species of animal and bird life, is the subject of this mural that occupies an entire wall of Young's Market in Westwood. A row of windows in the building are utilized as part of the mural, creating an effect of light and space.

❻ Dad Popcorn

"Dad Popcorn," 38'W x 12'H, 1992
Artist: Ben Barker
Location: 800 Main St., Susanville, CA

Every town has its beloved eccentrics and William M. Vellenworth, who came to be known as "Dad Popcorn," belonged to Susanville. During the early part of the century, Vellenworth, who originally hailed from Australia, left his job as a ship's carpenter in San Francisco and joined bridge workers building the railroad between Fernley and Westwood.

After moving to Susanville, he took on odd carpentry jobs, building cabinets and furniture. In his spare time, he designed and eventually built a popcorn cart large enough for him to sit inside, out of the winter snow and summer heat and dispense popcorn for five cents a bag.

Local residents took up donations and helped him replace the wagon. He continued selling popcorn until his death at age 83 on May 4, 1934.

The photograph from which the mural was drawn was taken about 1916-1917, and as well as Dad Popcorn, features three other former Susanville residents: Francis Pierce, Kathryn Pierce and Harry Pierce, Jr.

In his younger years Dad Popcorn was reputed to sometimes "tie one on". Once after spending a particularly cold night in a drunken spree, he ended up with pneumonia, was hauled off the street, and taken to Lassen County Hospital. He nearly died from exposure and was warned by Dr. William Dozier that if he didn't quit drinking he would wind up in the grave. From that day forward, rumor has it, Doc Popcorn never touched another drop of liquor.

In February of 1929, Dad Popcorn's wagon exploded, seriously injuring him and destroying his business.

❼ Old Main Street Susanville

"Photographs of Old Main Street, Susanville," 33'W x 15'H, 1993
Artist: Sterling Hoffman
Location: 65 South Roop St., Susanville, CA (LMUD Building)

The bones of a town are its past. With the muted tones of an old photograph this mural depicts a wide street devoid of traffic, which suggests the sleepy, slow moving town that was once Susanville. Originally called Rooptown, after Isaac Roop, the first white settler of the area, it became Susanville in 1858. Today Main Street flashes with traffic lights as the cars and trucks rumble through town. The mural above captures a transitional period on Main Street with its presence of a horse buggy and early automobiles. This scene is from a 1918 photograph of Main and Lassen Streets.

To the right is a scene from 1936 showing an early day delivery truck making its stop at the Purity Market which was located on the corner of Main and Gay. Purity Employees pose proudly in front of their truck.

"Photographs of Old Main Street, Susanville, 1936," 33'W x 15'H, 1993
Artist: Sterling Hoffman
Location: 65 South Roop St., Susanville, CA (LMUD Building)

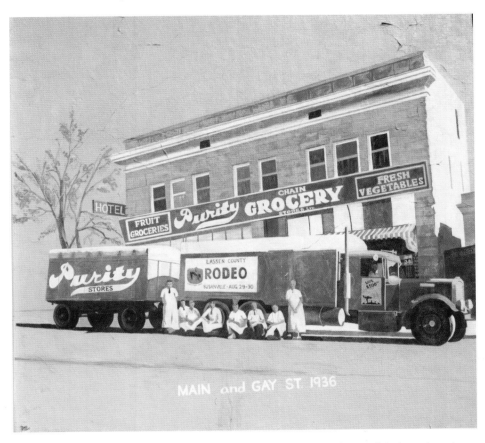

Sterling Hoffman was an avid art student throughout high school, and painted a small mural for his graduating class in 1986. In 1993, Sterling was attending Lassen College in graphic design when the Lassen County Arts Council contacted him to paint the "Old Main Street" mural, with funding through the Job Training Partnership Act (JTPA). Sterling employed several high school students, ages 17-18, in creating the two murals, using a grid system and a shading "value scale" from black to gray to white.

⑧ Susanville's Founder, Isaac Roop and his Daughter

"Susanville's Founder, Issac Roop and his Daughter Susan," 70'W x18'H, 1989
Artists: Ben and Leanna Lord Barker
Location: 700 Main Street (The Nathan Building), Susanville, CA

When Isaac Roop's wife died of typhoid fever in Ohio, he left his children with their grandparents and came to California. Susan was born in November, 1841, and joined him in 1862. He set up a homestead in the Honey Lake Valley which lies east of the Sierra Nevada mountains, eventually naming the town that would rise around him, Susanville, in honor of his daughter.

Each year on March 13, Isaac Roop's birthday, school children from throughout Lassen County descend on Main Street, Susanville to visit the town's murals. Beginning with the portrait of Isaac and Susan Roop, ending at Roop's Fort where Isaac and Susan first made their home, they learn about an early part of Susanville's history.

The mural of Isaac and Susan Roop was the first of many contributions created by Ben and Leanna Barker to demonstrate their deep commitment toward their community. After the mural's completion in 1989, Ben and Leanna continued to share their ideas and creativity in other murals throughout the town.

In 1998 Ben Barker died. His death left a hole in the community, and yet the deep love that many felt for him, from his wife and family to students, fellow artists and community members, keeps his vision alive. His art, which has become as much a part of the community as the buildings it adorns, affirms that Ben, like Isaac Roop, is an integral part of the spirit that makes up Susanville.

⑨ Mr. Eastman

"Mr. Eastman ," 26'W x 14'H, 1993
Artist: Arthur Mortimer, et al
Location: 802 Main St., Susanville, CA

The Mr. Eastman mural brings a part of Susanville's history into present time. It features two scenes from the life of Jervie Eastman (not to be confused with the Eastman of Eastman-Kodak) who founded Susanville's Eastman Photography Company in the 1920's.

The mural was designed by Arthur Mortimer and included several painters from Lassen Community College as assistants. The central setting of the mural shows Mr. Eastman reclining against his Model T Ford which he used to transport his equipment to photographic shoots. His original photographs captured California historical scenes, and became popular postcards of the time. The Eastman photographs have been acquired by the University of California, Davis and are available online at http://www.oac.cdlib.org/findaid/ark:/13030/tf6w100646.

"Cattle Ranching in Lassen County ," 64'W x 12'H, 1992
Artist: Arthur Mortimer
Location: 600 Main St., Susanville, CA

Muralist Arthur Mortimer designed the mural "Ranching in Lassen County" to depict the history of the ranching industry from past to present and, as nearly as can be predicted, where the industry might go in the future.

With open ranges, the need to brand herds with each ranch's identifying stamp is as important today as it was in the past; one section of the mural is devoted to the different brands used by local ranches over the years. A few of these brands can still be seen on the range today.

Arthur Mortimer resides in Santa Monica, California and has been painting murals since 1971. Most of his work is in or around Los Angeles, but he has traveled as far away as New York City to paint a 35 foot by 138 foot California-inspired mural on the side of Bloomingdales Department Store. His work has been widely shown in art competitions and exhibitions around the United States. While working on "Ranching in Lassen County" Mortimer lived here and took part in the Susanville community. He said, "I enjoy going into a community and learning about it, meeting the people and becoming a part of the community for a while."

⑪ Logging with Big Wheels

"Logging with Big Wheels ," 23'H x 17'W
Coordinator: Ben Barker, Artists: Local residents
Location, 705 Cottage Street, Susanville, CA

Logging is an integral part of Lassen County's past. Even today, trucks hauling Douglas fir down from the mountains sweep through Susanville. Once a lumber town, the last remaining mill closed in 2004. "Logging With Big Wheels" pays tribute to the county's roots in lumber. The mural, painted in the sepia tones of an old photograph, is one of the smaller ones in town and is located at the corner of Lassen and Cottage Streets. Huge, horse-drawn big wheel wagons were used in the early days of logging to drag logs over the rough forest floor. The picture shows these big wheels dwarfing grim-faced and bearded loggers beside them. Coordinated by Ben Barker, "Logging With Big Wheels" was a group effort by students in a mural painting class at Lassen Community College. In all, 13 people were involved in the project, including a 16-year old high school student who had never painted before and a 69-year old artist from Janesville. Another participant was a young man who is legally blind but able to see at close distances. Truly a community effort by a dedicated group of student painters, the mural was completed in a record time of three weeks.

⓬ Our Community History

"Our Community History,"20'W x 10'H, 1986
Location: , 845 Joaquin, Susanville, CA Ranchiera Gymnasium
Project Coordinator: Jean LaMarr, F. LaMarr, R. LaMarr, K. Curtis
Painted by: Herb Pesto

The history of three Honey Lake tribes: Paiute, Pit River and Maidu are illustrated in this mural located at the entry of the Rancheria gymnasium in the Joaquin Memorial Center. Coordinated by Jean La Marr, the project was completed by approximately fifteen young artists from ages seven through seventeen. The mural emphasizes the history not taught in school books. To learn this history, La Marr and her students spent much time with the Rancheria's elders gathering oral histories.

The bottom part of the mural revolves around coyote stories, which by tradition can only be told during the winter months. Many of the elders could not remember an entire story or could only tell it in the Indian language from which it originated. La Marr believes one of the main benefits of the mural is the educational value it will have for the Rancheria's children.

⑬ Honey Lake

"Honey Lake," 20'W x 16H
Artist: Jean LaMarr
Location: Susanville Rancheria gymnasium

Once Lake Lahontan, a huge inland sea, covered most of western Nevada and parts of California. About 8,000 years ago Lake Lahontan began receding, leaving behind reminders of what it had once been in the forms of Honey Lake and Nevada's Pyramid Lake. The Rancheria's mural of Honey Lake reveals the shores of the lake in the days before European settlers came to the area. The scene shows a marked absence of people. The dwellings appear empty; there is no smoke from fires or other signs of life. The only human figure is a baby in a cradleboard leaning against a tree.

⓴ Children of Headstart

"Children of Headstart," 36'W x4'H, 1988
Artist Coordinator: Jean LaMarr
Location: Susanville Rancheria Gymnasium

 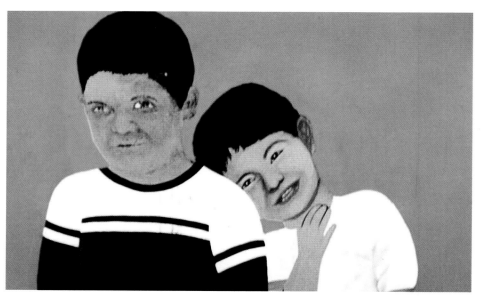

The photograph at the top of this page includes painted images of children seated on a bench, and actual children standing next to them. The standing children helped to paint the mural as a summer project. Jean LaMarr was influenced by the Mexican Mural Renaissance and its three major painters: Diego Rivera, Jose Clemente Orozco, and David Alfaro Sisqueiros. "Los Tres Grandes," used their artistic skills to chronicle the lives and struggles of the indigenous people of Mexico. This tradition has been the inspiration for many modern muralists, including Jean LaMarr.

The murals of the Rancheria continue this tradition by using art to educate, recover and chronicle the indigenous history of Lassen County for future generations. "Children of Headstart" pays homage to the most important link in keeping a community's history alive—the children who will grow up to pass on the knowledge they have learned from their elders.

⑮ Rice Canyon Petroglyphs

"Rice Canyon Petroglyphs," 19'W x 12'H
Artist: Michael McCabe
Location:, Susanville Rancheria Gymnasium

The earliest murals were most likely Paleolithic cave and rock paintings or carvings. Although their exact role is unknown, they appear to have been significant in the societies which created them. Some seem to have been part of daily life while others appear to have religious or ceremonial purposes. "Rice Canyon Petroglyphs" pays tribute to some of Lassen County's early rock carvings. Creating a petroglyph is time-consuming, and was probably accomplished by hunters while they waited for game to be drawn to the nearby water. First a sharp rock must be found, one that fits comfortably into the palm of the hand. Then comes the endless scraping. Many of the rocks in the Great Basin area are overlaid with a scaly, lichen-like covering, so the petroglyphs were not actually carved into stone but rather into this desert varnish which over the centuries has hardened, laminating itself permanently onto the rock. A man or woman would have had to sit patiently for hours or days tapping figures onto the surface.

At sunset in Rice Canyon the clouds turn magenta, and strange shadows leap up from the rocks. Birds of prey circle high above like flecks of dust. Just as at daybreak, the images take on a kind of life of their own. Maybe it has something to do with the changing light, those strange moments between light and dark, day and night, when some ancient magic, some essence of its creator seeps from the petroglyph. With fuschias and mauves, gold and red, in spirals and geometric designs, "Rice Canyon Petroglyphs" captures the essence of ancient magic and brings the petroglyphs to life once again. This mural was painted by Michael McCabe, a Santa Fe artist well known for his monoprints, who was visiting Susanville for the project.

⑯ Shadow Figures

"Shadow Figures," 19'W x12'H, 1988
Artist: Jean LaMarr
Location, Susanville, CA

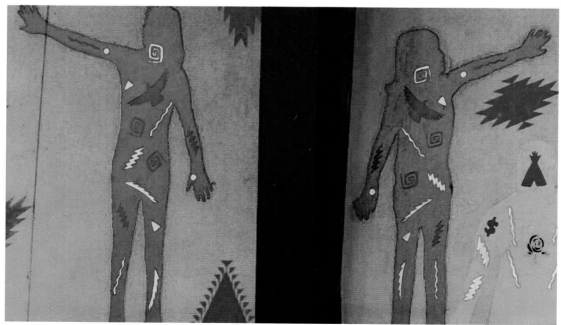

This mural was another summer project involving children of the Rancheria, who "froze" into favorite positions and had their silhouette traced on the wall. Each child also chose the petroglyph images to adorn their respective silhouettes and helped to paint them on. Jean LaMarr coordinated this project; she says that it was a way to provide meaningful summer employment for the children and to demonstrate to the children the connection between themselves and the public art they see.

The Susanville area is a place where several distinct native cultures intersect—Paiute from the Honey Lake Valley on the east, Maidu in the Sierra Nevada to the west, and Washoe to the south. Although each tribe followed different customs and had its own culture, they all shared a hunter-gatherer way of life and a religion based on shamanism. The overall effect of this mural is ethereal and transcendent, bringing to mind ancestors of a distant past or future generations yet to come.

49

"Wild Animals of Lassen County,"12 x4' , 1997
Artist: Joe Rees
Location: 2005 4th Street, Susanville, CA (McKinley Elementary
School)

Over the years, employment in Lassen County has shifted from logging and ranching to the government sector, especially in the Department of Corrections. Two large prisons sit on the outskirts of the city–the California Correctional Center (1963) and High Desert State Prison (1992). This mural was produced under the direction of Joe Rees, Artist Facilitator of the Arts-in-Corrections program. This artwork was the first in Lassen County to utilize digital manipulation to render a large piece.

1. Deer Mouse - 2. Striped Whipsnake - 3. Common Raven - 4. Western Tiger Swallowtail - 5. Golden-manteled Ground Squirrel - 6. Eagle - 7. Western Fence Lizard - 8. Western Toad - 9. Bobcat - 10. Yellow-bellied Sapsucker - 11. Ringtail - 12. Pacific Treefrog - 13. Steller's Jay - 14. Northern saw-whet Owl - 15. Porcupine - 16. Red Fox - 17. Blue Grouse - 18. Black Bear - 19. Coyote - 20. Mustang - 21. Swallow - 22. Pied-biled Grebe - 23. Raccoon - 24. Mountain Lion - 25. Mallard - 26. Northern Pacific Rattlesnake - 27. Pika - 28. Dove - 29. Northern Goshawk - 30. Striped Skunk - 31. Brush Rabbit - 32. Wild Turkey - 33. Mule Deer - 34. Mountain Quail - 35. River Otter - 36. Evening Grosbeak - 37. Black-headed Grosbeak.

⑱ The Castle

"The Castle," 41H x 9W', 1996
Artist Facilitator: Dianna Henning,
Location: 2005 4th St., Susanville, CA (McKinley Elementary School)

European murals may be seen as direct antecedents of the mural movement in the United States today. The earliest European murals were religious in nature, often painted on church walls and depicting biblical scenes meant as instruction for the illiterate parishioners. During the Renaissance, as Europe moved from a religious-dominated feudal culture to one motivated by capitalism, the subject matter of murals changed. Wealthy patrons often commissioned murals to be painted on living room and dining room walls of their baroque estates, using subjects inappropriate for church buildings. "The Castle" mural at McKinley Elementary School has a distinct European flavor. Designed by Dianna Henning, the mural bears the caption "The castle of knowledge is the castle of hope." A man leads a wagon across a bridge in a Medieval setting. Among the people to the side is a blue man to remind us that even in what appears ordinary, the unusual can be found.

"Dreams and Aspirations,"32Wx 8H' , 1996
Artist Facilitator: Dianna Henning
Contract Artist: Lori Collier
Location: 850 Richmond Road., Susanville, CA (Diamond View Middle School)

A collaboration between Diamond View Middle School and the California Correctional Center's Prison Arts Program resulted in this mural which shows where the students' dreams are taking them. The students came up with the ideas for the drawings. Under the direction of Dianna Henning, these drawings were then transferred to mural form by the inmates of CCC. They show a woman astronaut, miners, campers, writers and artists. The symbol of idealists and dreamers is also depicted in the figures of famous visionaries such as William Shakespeare, Martin Luther King, Albert Einstein and Emily Dickenson.

"World of Wildlife," 25'W x 7'H , 1995
Artist: Lori Collier
Location: Janesville Elementary School, Janesville, CA

One of the factors that makes murals truly pieces of public art is that they are community projects from their conception to creation to the final product. In "World of Wildlife," at Janesville school, the teachers and principal were as involved in the idea as were the artists and inmates who produced the piece. Under the direction of Artist Facilitator Dianna Henning at the California Correctional Center, the mural was conceptualized by Lori Collier, a Janesville artist who then supervised an inmate crew twice a week until it was completed.

This was the first mural produced under the Adopt-a-School program through the California Department of Corrections.

Working with inmates presents particular challenges. One of the obstacles at California Correctional Center is that because most of the inmates are in for short-term sentences, there is a high turnover in crews. Her inmate crew changed midway through this project and Collier had to finish the mural with an entirely different group.

The idea for this project was to create a mural that was both aesthetically pleasing and could be used as an educational tool for grade school children. The mural blends science, geography and art into a topographical map which shows some of the major wildlife of the continents and oceans.

㉑ Forest Service Mural I

"Forest Service Mural I," 16'W x 6'H , 1995
Artist: Ben Barker
Highway 36 at Eagle Lake Road, (Eagle Lake Ranger District Office)

The history of the early American West inevitably draws to mind images of covered wagons, mountain men and stunning scenery. Lassen County is an ecological transition zone. Sage, bitterbrush and tons of rust colored basalt and granite stretch over the hills that gradually change to scrub oak, juniper and Douglas fir. The ground is rocky and covered with brush. The scenery of the mountainous west is drawn together in this mural which depicts a group of early pioneers surrounded by fir trees while Mt. Lassen rises in the background. The covered wagon is drawn not by horses, but by cattle.

"Forest Service Mural II,"16'W x 6'H , 1996
Artist: Ben Barker
Highway 36 at Eagle Lake Road, (Eagle Lake Ranger District Office)

There is a flavor of the Italian fresco to this second mural in the Forest Service offices. Painted in a half oval, it is an idyllic, pastoral scene of a valley in autumn with an antelope in the foreground gazing on a line of covered wagons in the distance. Far off lies Eagle Lake. Once called Lake Acapsukati, the Indians of the area regard the lake as very ancient. Formed by lava flows which created the lake's jagged outline, Eagle Lake encompasses roughly 100 miles of shoreline and is the second largest natural lake in California. The lake has no outlets and no major streams feed into it. Eagle Lake is a popular local recreation area known for its abundant fishing, stunning beauty, and rich plant and animal life.

㉓ The Life of Eagles and Osprey

"The Life of Eagles and Osprey," 88' circumference x 14'H, 2000
Artist: Janet Fraser Dickman
Location: Ronald McDonald Water Tank, Osprey Overlook, Eagle Lake

The Osprey Lookout Site, a project of the Lassen National Forest, Eagle Lake Ranger District, combines both accessible and single-track hiking trails with a lookout area and a high point on the southeastern shore of Eagle Lake. It is a community resource, designed to provide osprey and eagle interpretation and viewing opportunities for site visitors.

Accentuating this interpretive site is "The Life of Eagles and Osprey" mural. Subtle in coloring, it blends with the natural surroundings of the landscape. Its subject matter depicts Osprey and Eagles, engaged in the daily activities of roosting, foraging, and caring for their young.

Janet Fraser Dickman's personal comments describe the essence of her experience with the creation of this water tank mural:

"This project was a very demanding one. Fighting the ever-changing elements made for difficult applications. All of my experience and knowledge was put to the test. The personal experience I gained was greater insight, enjoyment, and respect for the natural wildlife."

"As I painted this mural it was incredible to witness each living creature completing its mission in its own time and order. I was awed by the balance and structure of nature. My experience holds memories that will last a lifetime."

"Centennial Mural," 146'W x18'H, 2002
Artist: Janet Fraser Dickman
Location: 50 Grand Ave., Susanville, CA (Susanville Market)

The Susanville City Council commissioned the Centennial Mural to commemorate 100 years of the city's history. It depicts important historical scenes in Susanville from 1900 to 2000. The mural's location at Main and Grand is at the site where pioneers and their families would rest after crossing the desert on the Nobles Emmigrant Trail.

On the far left, a day hiker looks out over the modern-day city and reflects on its past. A freight train is shown hauling logs to Fruit Growers Mill, a major early industry that manufactured wooden fruit crates from local timber. Above the train is the Susanville Railroad Depot. This building has been restored and today serves as a visitor center and trailhead for the "Bizz Johnson Recreational Trail," a 26 mile hike/bike trail following the old rail line between Susanville and Westwood.

The Centennial Mural was designed and painted by Lassen County artist Janet Fraser Dickman, shown at right. This project was Janet's second major mural in the local area.

The building engulfed in flames is the Emerson Hotel, which once housed a store, bar, professional offices, a dining room, and a grand ballroom. The devastating fire of 1910 prompted creation of the city's first firehouse and watertower, pictured in the foreground. The Victorian-style building to the right of the fiery Emerson Hotel still sits at the top of Main Street. Originally built in the 1880's for Dr. Leonard, a dentist, it has been the Elks Lodge for many years.

Centennial Mural

Covered Wagons are shown travelling toward "Roops Fort", a log cabin built in 1852. This building is still standing, next to the Lassen Historical Museum on North Weatherlow Street. Shown on the canvas of the covered wagon at the left is a map of the Nobles' Emmigrant Trail, an early pioneer route in the Susanville area.

Centennial Commission
Gail Bengard • Lassen County Historical Society
Margie Teeter • Historic Uptown Susanville Association
Jim Jeskey • Susanville Rotary Club
Pete Margolies • Lassen County Times
Dee Ann Hunter • Susanville Rodeo Association
Jim Chapman • Lassen County Board of Supervisors
Doug Sayers • Susanville City Council
Dr. Francis Levier • Susanville Indian Rancheria

J. Newell Sorensen, City Administrator
Luann Rainey, Project Coordinator

MURAL SPONSORS

Susanville Supermarket • Rick and Anna Stewart

Lassen County Arts Council	Carol Jean Curry, CPA
NST Engineering	Jim Chapman, Lassen County Supervisor, District 2
Rocky and Gail Deal	D & L Distributing
Jim and Linda Wolcott	Rocky Crest Mobile Home Park
KSUE/JDX	Mr. & Mrs. James Brown
Lassen County Tobacco Coalition	Jim and Marilyn Chapman
Willits Motors, Susanville	Robert M. Barboza, Auto World
In Memory of Curt Willits	GFWC Monticola Club
Citizens Communications	In Memory of Les Vache
Tri Counties Bank	Noreen, Jesse, and Luke Frieling
Plumas Bank, Susanville	Bailey's The Handyman Can
California State Automobile Association	Richard and Leah Faye Bendix

Native Daughters of the Golden West, Parlor #152
Bank of America
Special Thanks
Michael R. Smith, General Contractor
Mike and Carolyn Smith
Bob Godman
Darrell Campbell

Susanville City Council • 2000
Mary A. Fahlen, Mayor
Lino P. Callegari, Mayor Pro Tem
Vernon Templeton, Council Member
Douglas Sayers, Council Member
Rodney E. De Boer, Council Member

The photograph above shows the muralist's clever use of the building's corner to show the front and side of the same wagon. At the right is the plaque recognizing the artist and the numerous sponsors of the Centennial Mural. Today, as in times gone by, a major project was accomplished through the collaborative efforts of many individuals and groups.

Creators of This Book

Jordan Clary, Writer
"Murals of Lassen County"
Jordan Clary wrote much of the text describing the murals and the artists who created them. Jordan grew up in Ohio and for the past twenty-five years has lived in various locations throughout the western United States and especially California. For seven years she lived in Lassen County were she was inspired and moved by the stunning beaty and vastness of the area. She describes it as a privilege to have worked on this book. By learning about the geography, history and personalities who have left their mark on Lassen County, she feels that her time here was greatly enriched. Jordan continues to write and publish poetry, fiction and essays in a number of venues such as literary journals, anthologies and the internet. She lives in southern California with her husband and youngest son. (Photo: Debby Schaefer)

Ron Garrelts, Photographer
"Murals of Lassen County"

A resident of Lassen County since 1971, Ron Garrlets began photography classes at Lassen College in 1989. He has had a number of one-man and group exhibits in California and Oregon, has won many awards, and has been published in several magazines over the years. Ron moved to Oregon in 2001, and upon his return in 2004, opened "Sudden Images" photography studio and art gallery in Susanville. "I want my photography to communicate not only images but emotions as well," says Ron.

Petra Rees, Graphic Designer, Artist
"Murals of Lassen County"

"In Europe where I grew up diverse cultures and languages surrounded me".

Petra Rees immigrated to the United States from Germany after she received a grant to study computer arts at San Francisco State University in 1986. In 1996 she moved to Lassen County where she worked as a teacher and art instructor at correctional facilities. "I have worked over the past 25 years in several genres, which include pencil, ink, paint, clay, photography, film, animation, video and glass."

Ben Barker, Artist, Teacher, and Driving Force behind
"Murals of Lassen County"

The late Ben Barker was the inspiration for the mural project and for this book. Ben taught art classes at Lassen Community College from 1981 until shortly before his passing in 1998. His first love was sculpture and he also taught classes in painting, drawing, jewelry making, and design. Ben felt that the murals project was a way to bring art and a sense of cultural identity to the entire community.

Mission

"To promote the arts in the educational, cultural, social, and economic enviroments, and to provide a voice for the artistic heritage and creativity of all Lassen County Residents."

History

In 1984, a diverse group of local artists joined together to establish a gallery to display their work. Over the span of several years, this group evolved into the Lassen County Arts Council, and their compass expanded to include all of the arts. The location of the gallery changed several times, but is now back at the original location on Cottage Street.

Activities

LCAC presents the work of local artists in its Cottage Street gallery, with showings that change monthly. Public school art classes frequently visit the gallery, and it is open to the public weekdays. Current and previous gallery shows are available for viewing at LCAC's website: *http://www.lassencountyarts.org*.

LCAC maintains an artist directory, and acts as a referral service: The Council can match up a string trio with an out

door wedding, or refer an inqury to a graphic artist for a special project. LCAC brings touring artists to the area through its "Artists in Residence" program. A performance group, say, a band of taicho drummers, will come to the area for three days, visit several of the area schools, perform for the children and involve them in learning about drumming, and culminate with a public performance on Friday evening.

LCAC sponsors the monthly "Words and Music" coffee house performances. LCAC has historically been funded through memberships, city and state subsidies, grants, and special event fundraisers.

Lassen County, California

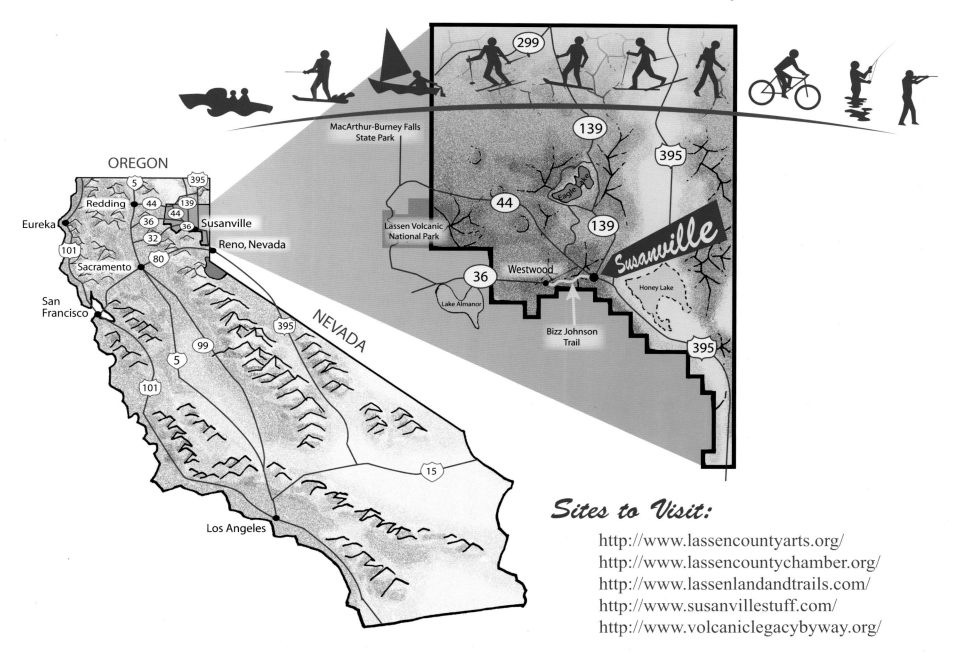

299

139

395

MacArthur-Burney Falls
State Park

OREGON

5

395

139

Redding

44

44

36

139

Eagle Lake

36

Susanville

Susanville

Eureka

32

101

Reno, Nevada

44

Lassen Volcanic
National Park

Sacramento

80

36

Westwood

Honey Lake

San
Francisco

Lake Almanor

Bizz Johnson
Trail

395

395

NEVADA

99

5

101

15

Los Angeles

Sites to Visit:

http://www.lassencountyarts.org/
http://www.lassencountychamber.org/
http://www.lassenlandandtrails.com/
http://www.susanvillestuff.com/
http://www.volcaniclegacybyway.org/